What's the Big Deal?

Why God Cares about Sex

STAN & BRENNA JONES

A NavPress resource published in alliance with Tyndale House Publishers

NavPress is the publishing ministry of The Navigators, an international Christian organization and leader in personal spiritual development. NavPress is committed to helping people grow spiritually and enjoy lives of meaning and hope through personal and group resources that are biblically rooted, culturally relevant, and highly practical.

For more information, visit NavPress.com.

What's the Big Deal?: Why God Cares about Sex

A NavPress resource published in alliance with Tyndale House Publishers

The Team for the Third Edition:
Don Pape, Publisher
Caitlyn Carlson, Developmental Editor
Elizabeth Schroll, Copy Editor
Jennifer Ghionzoli, Designer

For information about special discounts for bulk purchases, please contact Tyndale House Publishers at csresponse@tyndale.com, or call 1-855-277-9400.

Cataloging-in-Publication Data is available.

ISBN 978-1-63146-952-7

Printed in the United States of America

27 26 25 24
8 7 6 5 4

TO BRANDON, EMILY, CANON, AND BRADY

CONTENTS

ACKNOWLEDGMENTS

WE OFFER HEARTFELT THANKS TO the many parents who have shared their stories and perspectives, praise and disagreements about the content of the five-book God's Design for Sex series as we have spoken and taught about this subject around the country and around the world. Some of your stories have made it into the revised versions of these books!

We remain thankful for our friends mentioned in previous editions, with whom we shared the joys and travails of the journey of parenting our young children through to adulthood and with whom we shared enriching dialogue about the ideas in this book. Continuing thanks also to thirteen generations of graduate students in Stan's Human Sexuality summer course (1983–95), whose insightfulness, openness, and inquisitiveness so enriched our understanding of sexuality, and whose stories of how they learned (or mostly not) about sexuality in their families were an inspiration for these books. Revisions to the second-edition children's books were enriched by the professional reviews of Steve Gerali and Elaine Roberts; special thanks to Susan Martins Miller for her editorial expertise on that edition.

As we prepare the third edition of these books, there are many whose help we are grateful to acknowledge: We owe special thanks to Wheaton College for its support of the scholarship of its faculty, particularly in the form of a spring 2017 sabbatical. Stan was encouraged in 2011 by the opportunity and invitation by the editors of *Christianity Today* to share the essence of our approach in the pages of that important journal.[1] Emily Verseveldt served as an outstanding graduate research assistant 2014–15, gathering and updating a great deal of material for the *How and When* book; Emily, you are a model of organization and resourcefulness. Thanks also to Amy Smith, who has served as Stan's research assistant since 2017 and provided additional research and critical proofreading. Dr. Glynn Harrison, professor emeritus of psychiatry at University of Bristol, gave us the enormous gift of his review of and suggestions for the entire five-book series, for which he has our everlasting gratitude.

Each of our children's books benefited greatly from the editorial wisdom of Cathy Davis (for the original versions), and of Susan Martins Miller and Elaine Roberts (for the second edition). Lisa, Mark, and Anna McMinn read and gave very helpful feedback on early drafts of *What's the Big Deal?*

We are pleased to welcome Dr. Mark and Lori Yarhouse as current reviewers and future collaborators on this book series. Stan had the honor of contributing to Mark's training in clinical psychology at the master's and doctoral levels at Wheaton College, and together they have coauthored a number of articles and books. Since leaving Wheaton, Mark has established a distinguished career as perhaps the most prominent Christian psychological researcher in human sexuality in the world. Lori has invested her energies with Mark in parenting and home-schooling their three children. Our intent is that Mark and Lori will progressively become more involved with future revisions of the series. No one deserves deeper thanks than the Yarhouses for their extraordinarily helpful review of the entire five-book God's Design for Sex series in both the second and third revisions.

Special thanks to our NavPress editor, Caitlyn Carlson, and the publisher of NavPress, Don Pape, for your wisdom, friendship, and tremendous support. We are grateful as well for the partnership between NavPress and Tyndale House Publishers.

Finally, we want to express our deep love, appreciation, and pride for our three (now adult) children. Thank you for being our initial living laboratory for working out these ideas, for the shape and texture of your lives today, and for being so thoughtful, strong, and loving. Thank you for the wonderful spouses you brought into our family, whom we love as our own children, and for our dear grandchildren. You have, together and individually, enriched our lives far beyond what we ever could have imagined.

AN IMPORTANT WORD TO PARENTS

General Introduction to the God's Design for Sex Series

PARENTS, GOD GAVE you your sexuality as a precious gift. And you're reading this book because God has given you a child you love as a gift flowing from your sexuality.

God gave your child the gift of sexuality as well. If handled responsibly, this gift will be a source of blessing and delight. How can parents help make this happen?

Many forces will push children to make bad choices about sex based on false beliefs and values and on misplaced spiritual priorities. These forces are more powerful, confusing, persuasive, and ever present today than ever in history, thanks to the power of social media and the confusion of our culture. From their earliest years, children are bombarded with destructive, misleading messages—messages about the nature of sexual intimacy, about marriage, about family, about the boundaries of godly sexual expression, and even about the basic creational design of humanity as male and female.

These messages come from everywhere—through music, television, the Internet, discussions with their friends, school sex-education programs, and many other sources. The result? Confusion, doubt, and shame, as well as distressing rates of sexual experimentation, teen pregnancy, abortion, sexually transmitted disease, divorce, and devastated lives.

We believe that *God means for Christian parents to be their children's primary sex educators.* First messages are the most powerful—why wait until your child hears distorted views and then try to correct the misunderstanding? Sexuality is a beautiful gift—why not present it to your child the way God intended? God's Word is trustworthy and true—why not teach your child how to understand and live by its guidance in the area of sexuality? Why not establish yourself as the trusted expert to whom your child can turn to hear God's truth about sexuality?

The God's Design for Sex series is designed to help parents shape their children's character, particularly in the area of sexuality. Sex education in the family is less about giving biological information and more about *shaping your child's moral character.* The earlier you start helping your child see himself or herself as God does, including in the area of sexuality, the stronger your child will be as they enter the turbulent teenage years.

How and When to Tell Your Kids about Sex is a parents' resource manual in which we offer a comprehensive understanding of what parents can do to shape their children's sexual character. The four children's books in this series are designed for parents and children to work through together. Those books are structured to be read with your child at ages three to five (*The Story of Me*), five to eight (*Before I Was Born*), eight to twelve (*What's the Big Deal?*), and twelve to sixteen (*Facing the Facts*). These age ranges are not strict formulas; you need to exercise your judgment about your child's maturity level, environment, needs, and so forth to decide when and how to introduce the books.

The four children's books are meant to provide the foundational information kids need. Further, they are to be starting points for you to build upon and personalize as you discuss sexuality with your child in an age-appropriate manner. They provide an anchor point for discussions in order to jump-start deeper explorations. These books help break the silence and put the issues out on the table.

Don't simply hand these books to your child to read, *because our whole point is to empower you as the parent to shape your child's sexual character.* The books are meant to start and shape conversations between you and your child and to deepen your impact on your child in the area of sexuality.

In this series, we address controversial topics about which Christians disagree, including masturbation, how far people should go sexually when they're dating, contraception, gender identity, homosexuality, and more. Our goal in doing so is not to presumptuously present our answers as completely right but rather to encourage you to reach reasoned conclusions and to teach your child as you see fit before the Lord.

We have tried in each book to present information that we believe children of that age must have, without presenting controversial topics "too early." Your child may be confronted with complicated and confusing issues at a much earlier age than you expect. In such cases, you can draw on our discussions in later books to inform your dialogue with your child. For instance, we hold off on discussion of sexual orientation until the book for eight-to-twelve-year-olds (*What's the Big Deal?*), and on discussion of gender identity and transgender issues until the book for twelve-to-sixteen-year-olds (*Facing the Facts*). But your child may need more basic information much earlier, and in such cases, we urge you to use or adapt material from this book and our books for older children to meet your child's needs.

Why start early? Because if you as the parent are not teaching your child about sexuality, your child will learn distorted lessons about sexuality from television, the Internet, and playground conversations. If you are silent on sex while the rest of the world is abuzz about it, your child will learn that you cannot help in this key area. If you teach godly, truthful, tactful, and appropriate lessons about sexuality, your child will trust you more and see you as a parent who tells the truth.

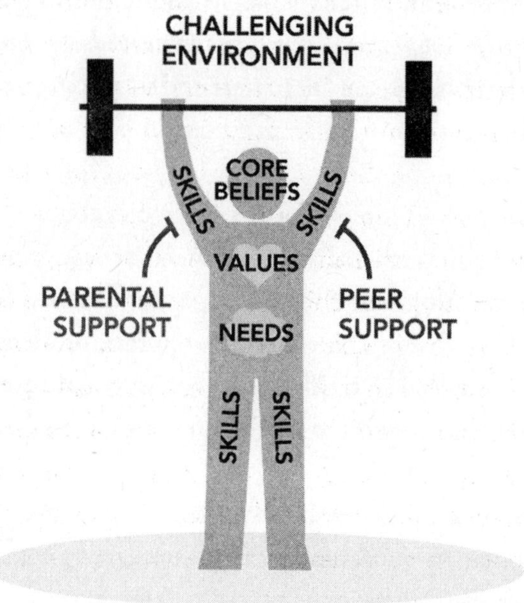

We'll briefly unpack each of the books at more length to help you discern which would be most helpful to you in your current parenting season.

PARENT RESOURCE:

How and When to Tell Your Kids about Sex:

A Lifelong Approach to Shaping Your Child's Sexual Character

This book is the parents' comprehensive resource manual for the God's Design for Sex series. We take on the hardest subjects, such as sexual abuse, gender identity, and homosexuality, helping you know when and how to bring up these subjects. Our goals for *How and When to Tell Your Kids about Sex* are to

- help you understand your role in shaping your child's character, including his or her views, attitudes, and beliefs about sexuality;
- instruct you in the twelve key principles for Christian sex education in the home and how to implement the strategies and tactics suggested by these principles;
- familiarize you with the challenges that your child will face from secular culture and empower you with strategies and skills to help them overcome those challenges;
- ground your understanding of God's view of our sexuality;
- equip you and your child to explain and defend the traditional Christian view of sexual morality in these modern times;
- examine each major developmental stage of your child's life and share age-appropriate information and approaches;
- address directly the most complex issues you and your child might or will face in today's culture in a manner grounded in biblical thinking and informed by the best contemporary science;
- explore how you can most powerfully influence your child to live a life of sexual chastity; and
- equip you to provide your child with the strengths necessary to stand by their commitment to traditional Christian morality.

As you read the following descriptions of each of the books for your child, please know that the concepts and issues presented in each of these books flow directly from the background provided by this foundational parents' guide.

AGES THREE TO FIVE

The Story of Me: *Babies, Bodies, and a Very Good God*

Your most important task with your young child is to lay a spiritual foundation for their understanding of sexuality. God loves the human body (and the whole human person), and the body is included in what God called "very good" (Genesis 1:31). Children's bodies, their existence as boys or girls, and also their sexual organs are gifts from God.

Young children can begin to develop a wondrous appreciation for God's marvelous gift of sexuality by understanding some of the basics of fetal development. In this book, we discuss the growth of a child inside a mother's body and the birth process. With such instruction, young children begin to develop a trust for God's law and to see God as a lawgiver who has the best interests of his people at heart. God is the giver of good gifts!

Finally, we want children to see families grounded on the lifelong marital union of one man and one woman as God's intended framework for the nurture and love of children. If you are reading the book as a single parent or with an adopted child, you will have opportunity to talk about how God sometimes creates and blesses alternative forms of families. We hope that you will find *The Story of Me* a wonderful starting point for discussing sexuality with your young child.

AGES FIVE TO EIGHT

Before I Was Born: ***God Knew My Name*** **by Carolyn Nystrom, with Stan and Brenna Jones**

Before I Was Born emphasizes the creational goodness of our bodies, our existence as men and women, and our sexual organs. This book introduces new topics as well, including the growth and changes boys and girls experience as they become men and women.

It includes a tactful but direct explanation of sexual intercourse between husbands and wives. God wants sexual intercourse limited to marriage, because sexual intercourse brings husbands and wives close together in a way that honors God and helps to build strong families.

Parents often ask, "Do my kids really need to know about sexual intercourse this early?" Remembering that you are the decision maker as to whether you use this book with a very mature five-year-old or with a more slowly maturing eight-year-old, the answer is yes. We believe this is a strategic decision parents must face based on their individual children, considering that first messages are always the most powerful messages. If, as a Christian parent, you want to begin to shape a godly attitude in your child about sex, why would you wait until they first soak in the misperceptions of the world? Why not build godly attitudes and views from the foundation up?

If you're reading this with an adopted child, use this opportunity to explain that not every couple will have biological children. If a baby doesn't grow in the wife's womb, the couple might look for a baby to adopt. And some women are not able to take care of a baby, so another family might adopt the baby and make it part of their family forever. Even though the baby grew inside a different mother, the husband and wife love this baby very much. Adoption is another way that God makes families.

AGES EIGHT TO TWELVE
What's the Big Deal?: *Why God Cares about Sex*

This book reinforces the messages of our first two children's books, covering the basics of sexual intercourse and the fundamental creational goodness of our sexuality. It continues the task of deliberately building children's understanding of why God intends sexual intercourse to be reserved for marriage.

This book goes further than the earlier books, adding more of the facts your child will need to know as they approach puberty. Further, it will help you begin the process of inoculating your child against the negative moral messages of the world. In *How and When to Tell Your Kids about Sex*, we argue that Christian parents should *not* try to completely shelter their children from the destructive moral messages of the world. If they mature in environments where they are not exposed to germs, children grow up with depleted immune systems that are ineffectual for resisting disease. When parents shelter their children too much, children are left naive and vulnerable; parents risk communicating that the negative messages of the world are so powerful that Christians cannot even talk about them.

But neither should you let your child be inundated with society's destructive messages. The principle of inoculation suggests that you should deliberately expose your child to the contrary moral messages they will hear from the world. It should be in your *home* that your child first learns that many people in our world do not believe in reserving sex for marriage, and it should be in your home that your child first understands such problems as pornography, teenage pregnancy, gay marriage, sexual identity and gender issues, and so forth. In this way, you can help build your child's defenses against departing from God's ways.

AGES TWELVE TO SIXTEEN

Facing the Facts: The Truth about Sex and You

Facing the Facts: The Truth about Sex and You builds upon all that has come before but also—in more depth—prepares your child for puberty. At this age, your child is old enough for more detailed information about the changes their body is about to go through and about the adult body they will soon receive as a gift from God.

In this book, your child will hear again about God's view of sexuality and about his loving and beautiful intentions for how this gift should be used. The distorted ways in which our world views sex must be clearly labeled, and your child must be prepared to face views and beliefs contrary to those they learn at home. We attempt to do all this while also talking about the many confusing feelings of puberty and early adolescence.

While children could read this book independently, we do not believe this would be optimal. We encourage you to read it alongside your child and then talk about it together. You could go chapter by chapter. Alternatively, you can read it and use it as a resource for important conversations with your soon-to-be or young teenager.

In this book, we address the most controversial topics of the series, topics about which biblically grounded Christians can and do frequently disagree. We make suggestions about appropriate moral positions on all of the important issues, including sexual-intimacy limits before marriage, masturbation, contraception, gender identity, homosexuality, and more.

We have joked that in each of these books, we are guaranteed to say something to lead almost any Christian parent to declare us too conservative or too liberal on some topic or to disagree with us somewhere. We do not presume our answers are completely right. At the very least, we hope our thoughts empower you, the parent, to think the matter through and present a better answer to your child as the Lord guides your thinking.

All of these books were written as if dialogue is an ongoing reality between mother, father, and child. Yet in some homes, only one parent is willing to talk about sex. Many Christian parents shoulder the responsibility of parenting alone due to separation, divorce, or death. Grandparents sometimes must raise their grandkids. We've tried to be sensitive to adoptive families and families that do not fit the mold of the traditional nuclear family, but we cannot anticipate or respond to all the unique needs of families. Use these books with creativity and discernment to meet the needs of your situation.

We hope these books will be valuable tools in raising a new generation of faithful Christian young people. If you follow this plan, we believe your child will have a healthy, positive, accepting, godly attitude about sexuality. As an unmarried person, your child will be more likely to live a confident, chaste life as a faithful witness to the work of Christ in their heart. If your child does marry, we believe they will have a greater chance of having a fulfilled, loving, rewarding life as a husband or wife. It is our prayer that this curriculum will encourage and equip you to dive into the wonderful work of shaping your child's sexual character.

CHAPTER 1

What's the Big Deal?

Suggestion to families: If your child is a good reader, ask him or her to read the parts where Sam and Amy are talking, while you, the parent, read the Mom and Dad parts. All of the material covered is important for both boys and girls. These written conversations will hopefully start even more conversations between your child and you about God's design for sex.

SAM: *Dad, what's the big deal about sex? Why do people talk and joke so much about sex, like on TV and stuff?*

DAD: It's confusing, but I will try to explain it as best I can. First, sex is a wonderful and beautiful gift from God. Beyond the many ways in which we are similar, God made men and women, girls and boys different from each other in marvelous ways. Our bodies are a gift from God. When husbands and wives share their bodies together in sexual intercourse, it is only one of the ways they share their love, but it is a special and powerful way. So sex is a big deal because sex is a marvelous gift from God.

SAM: *But that's not what I mean. People aren't talking about sex because it is a gift from God!*

DAD: I know! And I'm glad you are thinking about this enough to see that! But regardless of what others say, sex is important in everyone's life because God made us men and women with special and different bodies. God made sex, so it *is* a big deal.

But people make such a big deal about sex mostly for bad reasons, not good ones. For instance, sex is a big deal because when people don't use God's gift the right way, bad consequences often result. When people use the good gift of sex the way God meant it to be used, it is much more likely to have a beautiful and wonderful result. Sex is a big deal because so many people can be and are hurt by sex.

AMY: *Hurt by sex? How? What kinds of bad things can happen?*

MOM: Here's one example. Whenever a couple has sexual intercourse, the woman might get pregnant. A baby might start to grow in her womb. If the man and woman are married, usually this is a happy time. They feel like celebrating and it draws them even closer together in love.

But if the woman who has sex and gets pregnant is a fourteen-year-old girl, usually she is not happy. She may have to raise a baby without a husband. Her whole life changes—her dreams about finishing high school, dating, going to college; everything changes. God meant for pregnancy and giving birth to a child to be wonderful, something worth celebrating. But having a baby is something that many people dread because they didn't save sex for marriage.

DAD: Misusing God's gift of sex also spreads some diseases. Because sex brings people so close together, one partner can catch a disease the other partner has. Did you know that if a man and a woman never have sex with anyone except each other, that husband and wife have almost no chance of ever getting any diseases from sex at all? But because so many young people today are not waiting to get married before they have sex, these terrible diseases are becoming more common.

If you use God's gift correctly, treating it like a beautiful gift, you can be wonderfully happy that God made you a boy or a girl. But when people misuse sex, it almost always hurts someone. Did you know that hundreds and hundreds of thousands of teenage girls get pregnant every year? Did you know that many teenagers are getting sexual diseases with bad consequences like cancer or not being able to ever have children, all because they do not follow God's rules?

AMY: *That sounds terrible!*

MOM: Another reason sex is a big deal is that some people make it more important than it should be. Do you remember what the Bible says about idolatry? People commit idolatry when they take something God made and then treat it like it is a god. In the Old Testament, God hated it when people took things he made, like rocks and trees and gold, and then worshiped those things.

When people stop believing in the real God, they often start believing that other things can take God's place, things like money, or power, or being famous.

SAM: *Do people do that with sex?*

MOM: Sadly, yes. Sex is sort of like a god for some people today. They think that sex will make them happy or that sex is the most important thing in life.

They are wrong. Only God can make us truly happy, and only God deserves to be the most important thing in our lives. So when such people try to get happy by having as much sex as possible or by breaking God's rules about sex, they usually find they are not happy at all.

AMY: *I think I understand that, but why do people joke about sex so much?*

DAD: For some, it's because they want you to believe that sex is no big deal so that you might behave like they do, which would make them feel better about themselves. For others, it may be to cover up or express their disappointment in sex. In a lot of television shows and movies, people talk about sex, joke about sex, and think about sex all the time. I worry that these shows teach kids and grown-ups that sex is worth thinking about all the time. We Christians think sex is a wonderful gift, but it was not meant to take the place of God in our lives. And thinking about sex all the time or making sex the most important thing in our lives can never make us happy.

MOM: I agree that's why some grown-ups joke about sex, but I think there are different reasons, Sam, why kids your age joke about it. It's because they hear adults, especially on TV and in the movies, talk about it a lot, but the kids don't really know for sure what the adults are talking about or why. Maybe their parents haven't talked to them like we have with you. So the kids are really curious about it, but they're nervous and embarrassed because they don't really understand it. They also may joke about it because they don't understand how God made it special.

SAM: *That makes sense, sort of.*

DAD: But now let me tell you why I think sex needs to be a big deal for us. We want to teach you the truth about sex so that you will be ready to make the right decisions about it as a teenager and adult. Please always feel free to ask us any questions that come to your mind, because we won't be able to think of everything you need to know. And we won't always know the answers to your questions! We might need to think about it awhile before we answer you, but that's okay. We may even need to read to find the answer or ask someone, but we would be glad to do that. It is important for us to keep talking about this topic. We love you so much that we want you to learn about how God made us and meant for us to live, even when it isn't always easy to talk about.

SOME QUESTIONS TO DISCUSS

1. When have you heard kids joke about sex? Why do you think they do that?

2. What have you noticed about the way people in television and movies talk about sex?

3. What do you think about God making you a sexual person?

CHAPTER 2

Why Do People Do That?

SAM: *Dad, did you really mean it when you said I could ask you anything about sex?*

DAD: Yes, I did mean it. Sex is a gift from God, and I want you to understand that gift. So you can ask any question you have.

SAM: *Well, you and Mom told me that sexual intercourse is when a man puts his penis inside a woman's vagina. And I know that's how a baby gets made.*

DAD: That's right.

SAM: *I understand that people do that to have a baby. Do you have a baby every time you have sex? Why would people have sex if they don't want to have a baby?*

DAD: Those are great questions! The answer to your first question is no. People do not get pregnant with a baby every time they have sex. And here's why.

Remember how a man's body makes tiny little cells called sperm? One way of thinking of sperm is that they are sort of like seeds. If we were to take a seed from an apple, plant it in the ground, and treat it right, it might grow into a tall apple tree. It doesn't need anything else to become a tree.

But a sperm is different from a real seed because it can't grow into a human being by itself. A sperm is like half of a seed. To grow into a human being, it has to join with the other half. That other half is the egg, or ovum, that is inside the woman's body. When a man has sexual intercourse with his wife, a few drops of liquid come out of his penis, but in those drops are usually over 200 million sperm. So you can imagine how tiny sperm are.

When the sperm come out of a man's penis into the woman's vagina, the sperm begin to swim up into her womb to meet with an egg. You remember how a woman's vagina connects inside her body to her uterus, or womb? If the sperm swim up into her body and meet with an egg, a baby is created.

Although a man's body makes millions and millions of sperm, most of the time a woman's body releases only one egg each month. That egg is ready to meet with a sperm for only about one or two days out of the month. That means there are only a few days each month when a woman can get pregnant. If she has sexual intercourse any other day, she is not going to get pregnant. Most couples do not know for sure, though, exactly when the woman can get pregnant.

The sperm joining with the egg is really an amazing event. Did all that make sense?

SAM: *Yes, it made sense, but I still don't understand why people would have sex if they're not trying to have a baby.*

DAD: Okay. This is a little bit harder to explain. Sexual intercourse is not just for making babies. The Bible says that when a man and a woman have sexual intercourse, they become "one flesh" or "united into one." See, here in the first book of the Bible, it says, "Therefore a man shall leave his father and his mother and hold fast to his wife, and they shall become one flesh" (Genesis 2:24). And in the New Testament, Jesus repeats this truth with approval when he teaches about divorce in Matthew 19:5-6, as does Paul when he teaches about marriage, saying, "The two will become one flesh" (1 Corinthians 6:16).

God wants your mom and me to love each other very much and stay married all our lives. He wants us to create a home of love that will be a good place for children to be born, a place filled with love in which you and your sister can grow up.

AMY: *But that still doesn't tell us the reason people who are not trying to have a baby have sex!*

DAD: It's because God made sex so that it feels really good for both the man and the woman. Every man's penis is very sensitive. When a husband and wife have sexual intercourse, the feeling of his penis being in his wife's vagina is wonderful to him. And it feels wonderful for the woman as well, because God made her vagina and the area around her vagina very sensitive to pleasure, just like the man's penis. Not only that, God made a little spot just above the opening of the vagina that is called the clitoris. This little place on the woman's body is there only to give her pleasure from sex with her husband.

So sexual intercourse makes a husband and wife feel really good, and that helps them love each other more and more, because they are able to please each other and give each other great joy. Having sexual intercourse strengthens their love and draws them close together.

This is why many people call sexual intercourse "making love." If making love is loving and gentle and good, it helps the wife and husband love each other more.

AMY: *But what about people who are not married? Does it feel good to them?*

MOM: It can, but scientific research has shown that sex is better for people who are married and love each other than for people who are not married. And it has also shown that people who wait to have sex until they really know and love each other have more pleasure. Christians believe that sex should happen only in marriage and that everyone should wait until then.

SAM: *So do you and Mom have sex even when you aren't trying to have a baby? How much do you do it?*

DAD: Yes, we do. I don't want to tell you exactly how often we make love or when. That is a private matter between your mom and me. Some couples make love once or twice a week, while others enjoy making love more often, maybe four or five times a week, and some are happy doing it less often.

I am very thankful that your mom and I can have sexual intercourse together; it makes our love for each other stronger. Even when we are not trying to have a baby, having sexual intercourse expresses that I love your mom in a way that I don't love anyone else. It helps us be united together. And it feels good. Those are some of the reasons why we have sex when we aren't trying to have a baby. They're good reasons that make God happy. I'm thankful that God gave us this gift in our marriage.

SOME QUESTIONS TO DISCUSS

1. What do some other kids you know say about why people have sex?

2. What are the reasons why God made sex?

CHAPTER 3

Sex Outside of Marriage

AMY: *Mom, you know how you've always told us that sex is something that should happen only in marriage? That God only wants women to have sex with their husbands and men to have sex with their wives? If that's true, why does everybody on TV talk about having sex with boyfriends and girlfriends and even people they just met?*

MOM: Amy, I'm so thankful that you asked that question. TV shows often exaggerate things by focusing only on how *some* people behave and think.

Think about it this way: Dad just bought a new lawn mower. If Dad ignored the instructions that came with the lawn mower and tried to use it for cutting sticks and wood instead of grass, he would quickly find himself with a broken lawn mower. A broken mower will no longer cut grass like a lawn mower was designed to do.

God's gift of sex is like that. God gave this beautiful gift of sex with some instructions for how we should use it. God's gift of sexual intercourse was meant to help a man and a woman stay married to each other all their lives and feel very close and in love. When people have sex outside of marriage, they are not following God's instructions. That may feel good in some ways, but it often creates problems.

AMY: *But why would they do it, then?*

MOM: For several reasons. First, people have sex outside of marriage because sex makes their bodies feel good. Sometimes that makes them happy for a little while. But some things that feel good are not good to do. It tastes good to stuff yourself with your favorite candy, but that could make you sick. When you are mad, it might feel good to hit or hurt another person, but that doesn't make it right. The reason people take illegal drugs is because the drugs make them feel good, but taking drugs destroys your life rather than making it better.

A lot of teenagers who have sex to feel good do that because their lives are kind of empty. They are confused about why they are living at all. Isn't it sad that they don't know how much God loves them? God made them to have a wonderful life as his son or daughter, living the way that he knows is best for them.

Many kids today think that their lives have no meaning at all. When they become teenagers, they may think that having sex is just one more way to have as much fun as they can. And just like for those who take drugs, the fact that sex can be dangerous and harmful for you makes it seem that much more exciting for some kids.

AMY: *Well, that doesn't seem smart.*

MOM: It's not! Another reason why unmarried people have sex is that they use sex as a way of showing that they like or care for someone. In fact, I think this is one of the most common reasons.

We talked before about how many people call sex "making love." Sexual intercourse between a husband and a wife really is a way of "making love." Married couples have sex with one another because they love each other. Sex helps them be closer and love each other more.

But many people who have sex when they aren't married don't really love each other. They may like each other and get excited about each other, but real love is something that grows over time, and real love means they promise to stay together for all their lives. Waiting to have sex is an expression of real love, because it is the best way to seek God's very best for you and the men you will someday date, including the man you may one day marry.

AMY: *What if all your friends are doing it?*

MOM: One of the worst reasons to have sex is because friends pressure you to. It won't be long before you are in middle school, and soon after that, you will be in high school. Some people will say you are not a real woman if you don't have sex, that there is something wrong with you if you don't have sex, that you must prove you deserve being with the popular group by having sex. Those things aren't true.

Some kids can't stand it if other kids don't think they're cool. Some kids are so lonely or so confused that they will do whatever other kids are doing just so they won't be different. I hope you will be stronger and wiser than that. You don't have to prove anything to anyone by having sex.

You can see that these are not good reasons for having sex before marriage. Even so, by the time they leave high school, well over half of teenagers have had sex at least one time, and many have chosen to have sex often and with many partners. You will need to be very strong and know exactly what you believe if you are going to live the best way, the way God wants you to.

AMY: *I don't want to have sex before I am married. I want sex to be a good thing and not a bad thing.*

MOM: Good for you! You are already making wise choices. Let me warn you about one other thing. Even if a boy and a girl don't have sex, they can still do things with their bodies that can hurt them and that God does not want them to do. Some boys and girls share too much of their bodies with each other. For instance, they touch each other's bodies for the pleasure it brings or to be cool.

Staying pure like God desires for you means not sharing your body with another person until you are married. If you are modest and preserve the privacy of your body, you will make wise decisions that will help you have a blessed marriage later.

SOME QUESTIONS TO DISCUSS

1. What are some bad or false reasons for having sex?
2. Can you think of times when other kids tried to get you to do something that you knew was wrong, that you weren't supposed to do?
3. How can you stay strong to do what is right when others want you to do what is wrong?

CHAPTER 4

What Does God Really Say about It?

Dear Amy and Sam,

You two have asked some good questions lately about your bodies and about sex. We know that one of the scariest things about becoming an adult is that you will begin choosing for yourself what you really believe and making decisions that will affect the rest of your life. For the rest of your life, people will tell you all sorts of different things about what is right, what will make you happy, and how you should live. You will have to choose who to believe as you make these important decisions, because not everyone can be right!

We are trying to teach you God's ways, and the Bible is where we can learn about God's ways. Here are some verses from the Bible for you to read. We have written them down, along with some things for you to think about as you try to understand what these verses mean. Why don't you look up these verses in your Bibles? If you want, you can mark them so they will always be easy to find, because they are very important. Happy hunting!

After you read these verses, we can talk about any questions you might have.

Love,
Mom and Dad

PS: After the verses and our comments, we wrote down three reasons for saving sexual intercourse for marriage. We hope these ideas make sense to you.

DEUTERONOMY 10:12-13

(hint: this is toward the start of the Bible, in the Old Testament):

> And now, Israel, what does the LORD your God require of you, but to fear the LORD your God, to walk in all his ways, to love him, to serve the LORD your God with all your heart and with all your soul, and to keep the commandments and statutes of the LORD, which I am commanding you today for your good?

What beautiful verses! What God wants from us is simple: He wants us to fear him, live rightly by obeying his commands, love him, and serve him. By "fear the LORD," the Bible means to respect God and recognize that he has incredible power and goodness way beyond ours. But notice the last three words in the verse: God's commands are given for our good. He had our well-being in mind when giving his commandments to us.

PROVERBS 3:5-6

(hint: this is near the middle of the Bible, in the Old Testament):

> Trust in the LORD with all your heart,
> and do not lean on your own understanding.
> In all your ways acknowledge him,
> and he will make straight your paths.

This means that our own insights or ideas, and the ideas of people around us, can lead us the wrong way. But God's truth is like a perfect map that will always guide us on a good, straight road. God's truth will help us live our lives in the way that's best for us, that will make us the happiest we can ever hope to be. So if God's truth is the best guide for our lives, then we should ask what God says about sex, including who we should have sex with and when. God says in the Bible that only people who are married to each other should have sex.

1 CORINTHIANS 6:13, 18-20
(hint: this is in the New Testament):

> The body is not meant for sexual immorality, but for the Lord, and the Lord for the body. . . . Flee from sexual immorality. Every other sin a person commits is outside the body, but the sexually immoral person sins against his own body. Or do you not know that your body is a temple of the Holy Spirit within you, whom you have from God? You are not your own, for you were bought with a price. So glorify God in your body.

In the Bible, the word translated as "sexual immorality" means anything that is sexually wrong, particularly sex with anyone other than your husband or wife. God doesn't just say, "Don't do it." Instead, he says, "Run away from it!" That means you should run away from sexual immorality like you are running away from a robber or a fire! How important do you think it must be to God for us to not have sex before marriage if we should run away from it? And isn't it interesting that our bodies were made for God, and we can honor God by what we do with our bodies?

1 THESSALONIANS 4:3-5, 7
(hint: this book is six books after 1 Corinthians):

> For this is the will of God, your sanctification: that you abstain from sexual immorality; that each one of you know how to control his own body in holiness and honor, not in the passion of lust like the Gentiles who do not know God. . . . For God has not called us for impurity, but in holiness.

This passage and the 1 Corinthians passage are only two of the many places in the Bible where God says that sex outside of marriage is wrong. The apostle Paul here shows us that there are two basic ways to live our lives. One way, God calls holy, honorable, and pure, and this way of life requires honoring God with our bodies and staying away from sinful sex. The other way, Paul calls lustful, dishonorable, and impure; this is how God views sexual sin.

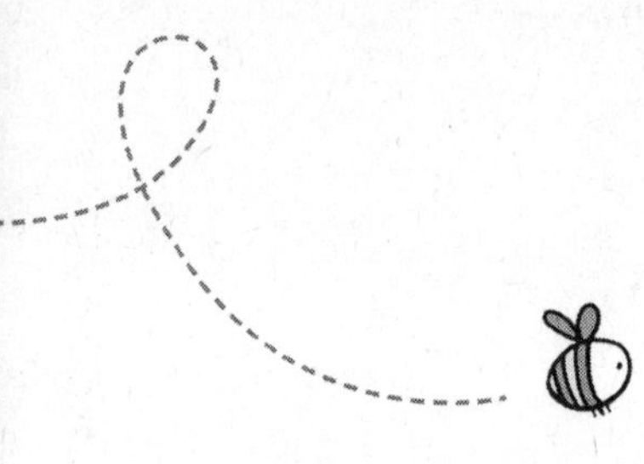

HEBREWS 13:4
(hint: this book is a few books after 1 Thessalonians):

> Let marriage be held in honor among all, and let the marriage bed be undefiled, for God will judge the sexually immoral and adulterous.

God doesn't just put up with marriage; he made marriage to be a great good, and so we should hold marriage "in honor." This is one of the many places in the Bible that says that God's gift of sex between a wife and husband is special and meant to be shared only between the two of them. When husbands and wives use God's gift of sex the way that God wants, they are keeping God's gift pure. That will make them happy, and God, too!

Writing these verses down helped us see that there are three main reasons to save sex to share only with your husband or wife.

1. We should save sex for marriage because God told us that is what he made sex for. God says sexual intercourse was created to help make a wife and a husband, two separate people, become "united as one" or "one flesh," to glue them together for life and help them have a better and more loving marriage. A husband and wife have the joy of having one special person they can be close to, glued to, for all of life. Sex with your husband or wife can be part of the glue that helps hold you together.

2. We should follow God's rules because he wants us to. Obeying those rules is a way of showing God that we love him. Jesus said, "If you love me, you will keep my commandments. . . . If anyone loves me, he will keep my word" (John 14:15, 23). If you said you loved us, but you never obeyed us, we would have a hard time believing that you really did love us. God wants us to love and trust him enough to obey him.

3. We should save sex for marriage because God's plan is the best plan for our lives. It is the way that will bring us the most happiness. People who break God's rules take big chances of hurting themselves by getting pregnant when they shouldn't, by catching diseases, and by being less able to have a good marriage. When we follow God's rules, we protect ourselves from harm and prepare ourselves to enjoy the good things God wants to give us in our lives. God gave both our sexuality and his commandments for our good!

These are three good reasons to follow God's ways!

SOME QUESTIONS TO DISCUSS

1. How is God's Word, the Bible, like a map for our lives?

2. What does the Bible say about having sex with someone other than your husband or wife?

CHAPTER 5

The Changes of Puberty for Girls

AMY: *Mom, there's something that I just don't get. I want to get married someday and be a mom, but right now I don't really like boys that much. How come girls start liking boys so much when they are teenagers?*

MOM: You know, I remember feeling just like you do. I remember thinking in third and fourth grades that kissing a boy would be really awful. I remember wondering why my older brother and sister seemed so crazy about dating. I especially remember when my older sister was sure that she was in love with some boy. She wrote his name over and over again and wanted desperately for him to call. I just didn't get it! Why was she so crazy about boys?

AMY: *That is exactly what I mean. Why does it change?*

MOM: It's still a real mystery to me, too, how it happens. But I'll tell you something: It's a wonderful thing that both young men and young women can feel that another person is so very special. God made us so that as we grow up, we don't want to be alone. Instead, we want to have a special someone we can share the rest of our lives with. God made you so that you can fall in love with that man.

Dad and I love you very much, and when you were a baby, our love was about all you needed. But after a while, you still wanted our love but also wanted to have friends, too. And there will come a point, when you become a young woman, when the love of your mom and dad, and even of friends, won't be enough anymore. You will feel a desire to love someone special. In fact, you will feel ready to fall in love.

I think God gave us this gift for a lot of different reasons. Being able to fall in love makes it possible to have one of the greatest gifts that God can ever give—a good marriage. For a good marriage to work, it must be filled with love. A loving marriage may give you the chance to have children and to pass your love on to them. And being able to fall in love reminds every one of us that we were not made to be alone. It is like a reminder every day of our need for God.

Even if you don't get married, these feelings are still a big part of being a grown-up. Single people can live wonderful lives filled with special friendships and fill their desire for a special relationship with their love for God and with their friendships. A healthy single person continues to love their parents but wants to have a life independent of them.

AMY: *But how does it happen? How do your feelings change so much?*

MOM: Part of the change happens in our hearts and minds and feelings, and part of it occurs in our bodies. Our bodies and our feelings are connected together in a marvelous way. The part that's in our hearts and minds and feelings happens when you are ready to be an adult and to have a special person to share your life with. You don't want to be taken care of like a child anymore. Instead, you feel ready to get out more on your own and live your own life.

But I'll tell you a secret: Being an adult can be a bit lonely and frightening sometimes. It's a big and scary world out there. But God loves us and wants to comfort us. Trusting him helps us not to be frightened of all the things that can happen in our world. It's also a gift from God when we can share our adult life with another person who is our partner.

You have already started to become an adult, though you have a way to go yet. When your feelings begin to change, and you begin to think, *I really like that boy*, you will know that you are beginning the wonderful transformation toward becoming a young woman. I am excited for you as you go through this, though it sure is a scary time, full of ups and downs.

AMY: *What about our bodies? You said our bodies are part of the change.*

MOM: That's right! You've heard about puberty already. Puberty is a period of two, three, or four years when your body will gradually change from being the body of a big kid to being the body of a developing adult. You will begin to grow more hair on your body, especially pubic hair right above your genitals. Puberty is the time when kids go through a real growth spurt and grow closer to the size they will eventually be as adults. A girl's muscles begin to grow and the shape of her body starts to look more like an adult woman's. Her breasts begin to develop, and she starts to wear a bra.

AMY: *What is that like?*

MOM: When it begins, you will feel hard little lumps under your nipples. Doctors call these "breast buds." But then pretty soon, the softer tissue begins to form under your nipples, and over a period of years your breasts get larger until they reach their full, adult size. For some women, their breasts are full size when they are fourteen or fifteen, but for others, it isn't until they are in their early twenties.

AMY: *Is growing hair all that happens to your genitals?*

MOM: No. Puberty is also the time when your sexual organs begin to change in wonderful ways that make them physically ready for you to have sexual intercourse and to become a parent. For young women, this means that the eggs in their ovaries mature and they begin to have their periods, which is a sure sign that their bodies are in the process of getting ready to become pregnant if they have sexual intercourse.

AMY: *What do we do to make those changes start?*

MOM: Nothing! You can't do anything to make the changes start earlier or later; they just happen when your body is ready. For some kids, the changes start early, around age ten or even earlier, and for others, they happen later, at age fourteen or fifteen or even later. What starts the whole puberty thing off, though, is that for some mysterious reason, our brains begin to tell our bodies to produce sex hormones. A woman's most important sex hormones are produced in her ovaries inside her abdomen, where her eggs are stored.

The hormones put out by a young woman's ovaries cause all these amazing changes in the body. These hormones also affect our brains. I remember once when I told you about sexual intercourse, you said, "That is so gross. I can't believe that people do that." But after these hormones begin to circulate all through your body, even in your brain, the things that sounded gross once upon a time will no longer sound so gross. In fact, they'll sound rather nice. These hormones don't make you have sex. But they do help you change so that it will begin to sound really nice to be close to a young man, or for a young man to be close to a young woman. Teenagers begin to have vague feelings that they just wish they could have sex, because the idea of it just sounds wonderful. They have these feelings even though they haven't ever had sex before and don't really know what it feels like at all.

AMY: *That must be really weird to change like that!*

MOM: It is! When all of this begins to happen to you, it will feel rather strange. I remember feeling really mixed up about it all. Without knowing why, I went from thinking boys were awful to thinking they weren't so bad to really hoping that one of them would like me because I sure did think he was wonderful. And for some reason, I felt totally embarrassed about the way my feelings were changing.

Boys and girls who are becoming men and women think about both love and sex a lot. You will probably feel stirrings of sexual attraction and excitement; these may come when you're thinking about a boy you find attractive or dream about a relationship with someone special.

Girls probably think more about the love part and boys more about the sex part when they are teenagers. Women young and old have been given a great gift that helps them think about the love aspect of relationships more than boys do: That is the gift of knowing instinctively and deeply that their bodies are made to carry and nourish new life inside of themselves. Because of our monthly periods, we are reminded constantly that our bodies are designed by God to bring forth new life, and we instinctively want to bear new life through a faithful love relationship with our husband, a relationship that will be lifelong and ideal for raising children.

Girls can think about sex by itself, too. Sometimes girls get sexually excited and can feel that their vagina is a little bit wet with the lubrication that goes along with being sexually aroused. There's nothing wrong with this; it can happen when you're thinking about an attractive boy or when you're daydreaming about a special relationship. When you feel this way, you can simply remind yourself that these feelings are a gift from God given for a purpose: namely, to contribute to a beautiful marriage later in life. By focusing on God's purposes for your sexual feelings, you can aspire to shape your thoughts and feelings in a way that honors God. In this way, you can gradually point yourself toward valuing what is good. I hope you can keep talking to me about this. If you are like me, this whole area will feel a little awful and embarrassing to talk about. That's okay—it makes it harder to talk, but it is perfectly normal to feel those feelings.

And remember: All this is happening because God is making you into something new, something you have never been before. He is changing you from being a child to being an adult. It doesn't always feel comfortable because God is not done with his changes. But you have to go through these changes to become the adult he wants you to be.[2]

SOME QUESTIONS TO DISCUSS

1. What do you think about the way God made your body to change and grow? Does it sound scary, exciting, or something else?
2. What things about being an adult do you most look forward to?

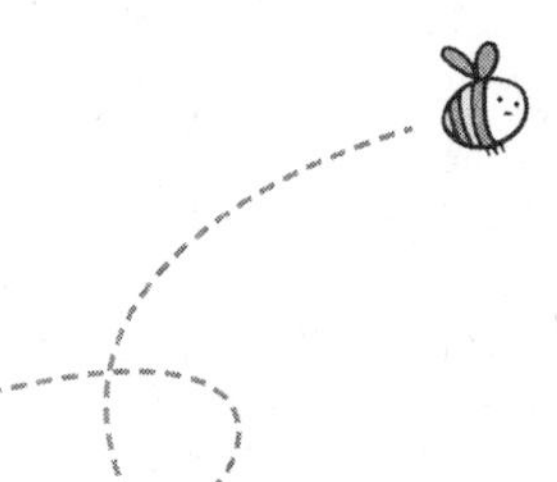

CHAPTER 6

What Is a Period?

AMY: *Mom, what is a period? I know it has something to do with a woman bleeding from her vagina, but it doesn't make sense to me. What is it?*

MOM: Remember how a new person is created when the sperm from a man joins with the egg from a woman inside of her body? The man's sperm gets inside the woman's body when they have sexual intercourse. What I haven't explained to you is how the baby lives and develops inside the mother's body.

AMY: *But Mom, what does that have to do with a period?*

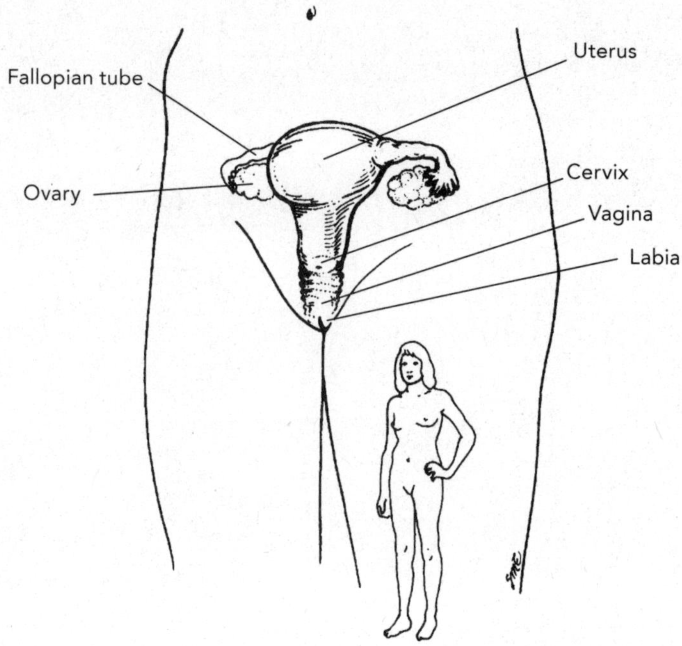

MOM: You'll see. The growing baby inside the woman's uterus draws all of its air, food, and water from its mother's blood through its umbilical cord. Your belly button is the scar left from where your umbilical cord attached to your body. It attached to my uterus at the other end through something called a placenta. To be able to feed a baby that starts off smaller that a grain of sand but winds up weighing more than six or seven pounds, the mother needs to have an extra-rich supply of blood in her uterus.

Just before the woman's egg is released each month, her uterus begins to build up this extra layer of blood vessels and cells and blood to get ready to feed her baby if she gets pregnant. When an egg or ovum is mature, it is released to travel toward her uterus through her fallopian tubes. If a woman has sexual intercourse with her husband around this time, her husband's sperm will have traveled from her vagina up through her uterus and into her fallopian tubes. So there's a chance she can get pregnant.

If the sperm and egg unite to become a baby, the woman's uterus continues to be richly supplied with blood that feeds the baby until it is born many months later. The woman's body is so amazingly sensitive that it usually knows within a few days after a sperm and an egg unite that she is pregnant. Her body knows long before doctors or even the woman herself can tell. But if she is not pregnant, this extra supply of cells and blood vessels is not needed to nourish the baby. It begins to break up and flow out of the woman's body. And this is what is called her menstrual period.

AMY: *That sounds awful!*

MOM: It's really not awful. I may have made it sound like a big event, but it's not, really. The uterus is small, only about the size of a small apple, so the amount of blood that a woman bleeds is not very much. For most women, it's only about four to six tablespoons over the whole three or four or five days her period lasts.

AMY: *Does it hurt? When I cut myself so that I bleed, it really hurts!*

MOM: This is really different than that. Your body knows it does not need this extra blood it built up, so it is just letting that go. Your body is not injured, like it is when you cut yourself.

How much it hurts is different for different women. For some women, there is no difference at all between the way they feel when they are going through their menstrual period and the way they feel at other times. Most women feel some discomfort in their stomach area around their uterus when they have their periods, and a few women even have painful cramps. There are some good medicines to help women who have discomfort and pain. Sometimes women feel more tired or headachy for a day or two during their period.

Your breasts may feel tender too. Any of these feelings are normal and nothing to worry about.

AMY: *I don't know, Mom. I don't think I'm going to like having a period.*

MOM: I remember feeling just that way. It can be a little awkward and embarrassing at first, but it just takes some getting used to, and then it's no big deal. There is nothing unhealthy or dirty about having your period. You simply have to learn to not let the little bit of blood get on your clothes and how to stay clean.

AMY: *How do you keep the blood off your clothes?*

MOM: There are two things we women use to do this. One is called a sanitary pad. It's just a thin pad of a cottony paper that you wear in your panties between your legs. The pad soaks up the little bit of blood and keeps you clean. The other way to stay clean is to use a tampon. A tampon is made of the same kind of stuff as the pad, except it is packed tighter in a shape like a small tube the size of a very short pencil, only about two inches long. A woman pushes the tampon gently into her vagina, and it soaks in the blood from her period there inside her vagina. The packages of pads and tampons contain careful instructions for how to use them. A girl must never try to push anything up into her vagina except a tampon, and we should talk about it before you try so I can answer any questions you might have. Many girls prefer to use pads rather than tampons. Many others, on the other hand, choose to use tampons when they are engaged in sports like gymnastics or swimming. There can be lots of situations in which using a tampon makes sense.

Having a menstrual period is a marvelous thing. It is a sign that the woman can get pregnant. It is a sign of how wonderfully God has made her body to carry life within it.

SOME QUESTIONS TO DISCUSS

1. What are some things you have heard about how girls start having their periods and what it is like for them?
2. How do you feel about someday starting your period?

CHAPTER 7

The Changes of Puberty for Boys

DAD: Sam, your mom had a talk with Amy about the changes that she could anticipate as she goes through puberty. Is it okay if I talk with you about those changes for boys?

SAM: *Sure, Dad. I know that puberty is something you go through to become a man, but I'm not sure what it is.*

DAD: Well, it is a little hard to explain because it's a bit different for everybody. It's especially difficult for boys because girls have a clear marker of when they have started puberty, and that's when they have their first period. For boys, it is not so clear. You know how you have been growing steadily ever since you were born?

SAM: *Yes, I needed new shoes last week because my old ones were too small!*

DAD: That's a great example. Well, you will have a growth spurt when you start puberty. But your body doesn't just get bigger and stronger; it also changes to make you ready to be a husband and father. It's almost like you have a clock inside your brain that suddenly tells your body to switch to adult mode.

When that signal comes, your testes begin to produce more testosterone, a hormone which has many effects as it circulates throughout your whole body. You have the growth spurt I mentioned, and you can build a lot more muscle and become much stronger.

For most boys, the first sign that they're going into puberty is that they grow a bit of darker hair right above the penis. This hair is called pubic hair. You begin to grow some in your armpits, too, and soon after, you begin to grow hair on your face, which usually begins when a few a wispy mustache hairs become visible. Some boys develop acne on their face, and their perspiration begins to smell stronger.

SAM: *I'd like to be stronger, but I'm not sure I want acne!*

DAD: It is hard to tell in advance whether you will have acne or not. I had some acne, but your mom had very little. You may be lucky and be like her in this area.

There are other changes as well. For instance, a boy's voice will begin to change, getting deeper as he matures. But beyond all of those changes, the biggest changes will happen in your brain and in your sexual organs. When your brain causes the testes to produce more testosterone, for the first time, your testes will begin producing sperm.

SAM: *Someone told me that sperm are like miniature babies that get planted in the mother's womb. Is that true?*

DAD: Not quite. Several ancient civilizations thought that. They thought that the woman's body was like good soil for the seed that came from the man. But actually, each sperm is incomplete, like half a seed that has to be joined with the other half that comes from the woman. When a sperm joins with the woman's egg to make a baby, that baby can then be nourished in the womb.

SAM: *I don't understand how you can have half a seed. What happens?*

DAD: The process is miraculously and incredibly complex. Every cell in our bodies has the same set of chromosomes, each made of thousands of genes. In the last century, some brilliant scientists discovered that each chromosome is structured sort of like a twisted ladder. Imagine a ladder leaning against a wall. The pieces on either side of the ladder that go straight up are the genes made up by a string of chemicals. The crossing rungs that you would step on to climb the ladder are like a chemical rope that holds the genes on either end together.

The genes on the side are arranged in different ways, forming a very complex code that tells your body how to grow up to be you. They direct one bunch of cells to become eyes, and another fingers; another sets the color of your hair, and on and on. Now, imagine the ladder is a mile high and twists like a corkscrew; that's how complex chromosomes are.

As if that wasn't enough of a miracle, listen to how we get half a seed. When your testes make sperm, the process begins by making cells that will become sperm, millions of them. Each cell initially has a copy of all your genes. Then a special set of chemicals cuts all the rungs of the ladder for each chromosome from one end to the other. It does this for every chromosome in that cell that is becoming a sperm. From each cell, two sperm are born, each with a complete set of half-ladders.

The same thing happens in the woman's body in her ovaries. Every egg in her body contains a complete set of half-ladders. Incredibly, when one sperm fertilizes an egg, these half-ladders connect together to make a new, complete set of ladders, the new chromosomes. Each one combines some of the characteristics of the father and some of the characteristics of the mother to make a unique human being!

SAM: *That is so complicated that I'm not sure I understand.*

DAD: Maybe that was too much detail, but I want you understand what a miracle it is that every baby is born unique. A big difference between men and women is this: A healthy man makes millions of sperm every day, but a healthy woman has only about 300,000 eggs when she goes through puberty, less than the number of sperm made in a man's body in a day. Every single egg she will ever have is in her ovaries at the time she's born. Her ovaries protect those eggs carefully for years. In contrast, your testes are creating millions of sperm every day, and constantly getting rid of the ones that die.

When your body begins to make sperm, you have the ability to contribute to making a baby. But you're certainly not ready yet.

SAM: *What makes me ready?*

DAD: Well, the added testosterone in your body helps you continue maturing physically, as I said; you get stronger, taller, grow more hair, and so forth for several more years before you are fully an adult. Your genitals change a bit too; your penis, testes, and scrotum get larger and a bit darker in color. Your pubic hair gets thicker. But the testosterone affects your brain as well.

I remember the first time I told you about sex, it did not sound appealing to you at all. And you had no interest in girls other than just being friends with some of them. As your brain changes during puberty, however, you begin having romantic and sexual attractions toward women. But along with these come all sorts of confusing new feelings. Boys go from thinking they can't stand girls to thinking they aren't so bad to thinking a lot about falling in love and having sex. It's easy to feel confused and embarrassed as these changes occur. And you start having erections.

SAM: *What's an erection?*

DAD: When a man has sexual feelings, his brain and body direct more blood into his penis—a lot more. His normal penis is smaller and very soft, but as more blood rushes in and less gets out, the spongy tissues of his penis hold the blood and make his penis harder and longer, so that sort of sticks up and out from his body.

SAM: *That sounds embarrassing! And weird.*

DAD: It can be embarrassing. As you begin to have more sexual feelings, some of the feelings are very strong and very confusing. You can have erections at very awkward times. I remember once being at a pool when I was thirteen. I saw a pretty girl—I didn't intentionally think about sex or anything, I just thought she was pretty—and suddenly, I had an erection. I just stayed in the pool, swimming around, until it went away.

SAM: *That sounds awful.*

DAD: Not everything about becoming an adult is easy, Sam. You will get through it. Another thing that can be embarrassing is what is called a wet dream. God made us men so that after puberty, we're likely to have several erections every night in our sleep, usually when we are dreaming. Usually you just have these erections for ten minutes or so and then your penis goes back to normal. But sometimes, your brain will trigger what is called an ejaculation, when fluid called semen is ejected from your penis. It's not a lot of fluid, only a teaspoon or so, but you will wake up and discover your underwear and possibly your pajamas or your sheets have a wet smear of fluid on them. This is perfectly normal, even if it can be embarrassing. You can just change your underwear or even your sheets; your mom and I understand that this just happens.

SAM: *It sounds almost like wetting the bed! How embarrassing. Why does that happen? And what is semen? Is that another name for sperm?*

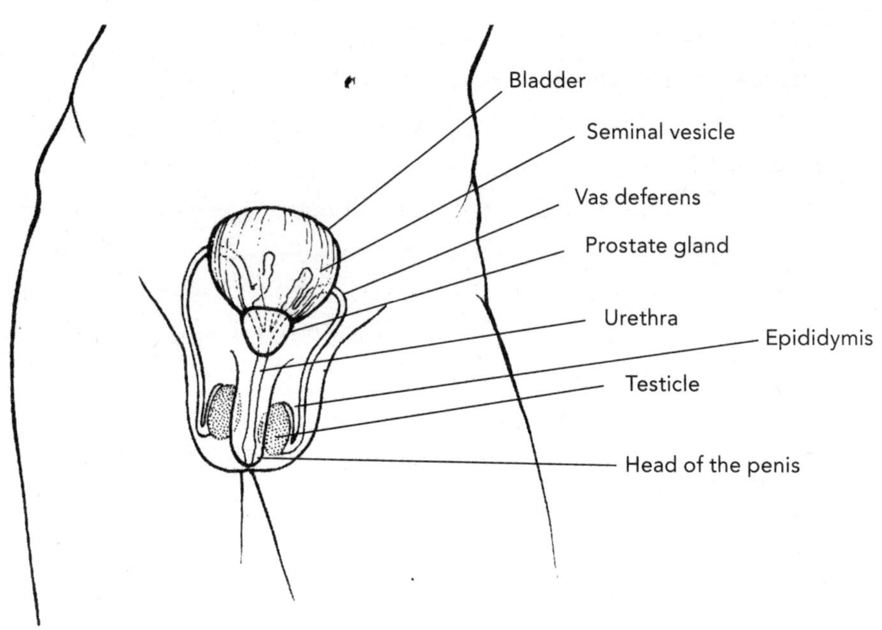

DAD: Again, don't be embarrassed, because we understand. It's all just a normal part of becoming a man. And while wetting the bed is a sign of not being mature, having wet dreams is a sign of becoming mature.

Why does it happen? I think it is because your penis becomes more sensitive to pleasure as you go through puberty, and your brain puts those feelings together with thoughts in your dreams—thoughts that you cannot control—and all these things combined cause your body to have what is called an orgasm. An orgasm is the name we use for an ejaculation of semen combined with the sudden burst of pleasure that goes along with it.

SAM: *But I still don't know what semen is.*

DAD: Semen is sperm mixed together with some other protective fluids. Let me explain how it happens.

When an ejaculation is triggered by the brain, it starts with the sperm. Those sperm have been produced in the testes and stored in what is called an epididymis, which is right next to each testicle. The sperm move very quickly through two tubes called the vas deferens to a spot right under the bladder. There, in the prostate gland, the sperm are combined with some other fluids from the prostate itself and other tiny glands, the seminal vesicles, to become semen. These extra fluids help keep the sperm alive. All this happens in seconds, and the semen containing sperm is pushed out of your urethra at the end of your penis. And that's how an ejaculation happens.

SAM: *That's complicated.*

DAD: It is. God made our bodies amazingly intricate and complex. Don't worry about the details, though. We have plenty of time to talk about it again. But remember, our feelings are just as important as the physical facts.

I want you to understand that as you go through puberty, your sexual feelings will be very strong. The power of the hormone testosterone on your body, a body that's not used to it, causes you to have strong and sometimes confusing feelings at awkward times.

SAM: *Confusing how?*

DAD: Well, you may find yourself having sexual feelings toward a girl that you really like and think you might love. This can seem normal, though a bit awkward. But you could also feel sexually excited for no apparent reason, or at a time you don't want to feel that way. Boys can feel attracted to adults like movie actresses or women you see in advertisements, or you can experience sexual feelings thinking about another boy or man who is handsome or you admire. You can feel excitement when you hear somebody describe something you know is wrong, like when somebody talks about forcing a woman to have sex.

Sam, this is where everything we have taught you and what you believe makes a huge difference for your future. When sexual feelings come unexpectedly, like they do when we are sleeping or just happen during the day, your decisions of how you handle them shape the man you will be in the future.

The sexual feelings can just happen, but you then choose whether to think further about it or to let it go. If you make a habit of encouraging and strengthening sexual feelings in ways that dishonor God and against what we have taught you about saving sex for marriage, you'll be gradually pointing yourself toward desiring things that God sees as evil and twisted.

SAM: *How do I go in the right direction?*

DAD: That may be the best question you have ever asked. And the best answer I can give is to love and trust God, read the Bible, follow the words and commands of Jesus, and talk to me or other mature Christians who gone through the very same things that you will be going through. And please know that I will be praying every day that God will steer and guide you in the right direction as you seek to follow him.[3]

SOME QUESTIONS TO DISCUSS

1. How do your friends think about relationships with girls? How do older boys tend to think about it?
2. What do you most look forward to about growing up? What do you feel anxious or fearful about?

CHAPTER 8

But Why Can't I Do That?

SAM: *Dad, you know how you won't let us watch movies or TV programs that have sex in them? Like R-rated movies?*

DAD: Yes, it's very important to your mom and me that your sister and you not see things like that. Why are you thinking about that?

SAM: *Some of the kids at school get to watch movies like that all the time. Their parents have cable television and don't really care what they watch. Some of the movies sound really cool.*

DAD: Do you wish you could see those movies because other kids talk about them?

SAM: *Well, sort of. I don't want to watch anything that's dirty or bad, but some of the movies just sound really great the way other kids describe them. I just don't understand.*

DAD: I'm really glad you wanted to talk with me about it. I'll try to tell you what I think about this. Then, even though I'm not very likely to change my mind, I really want you to tell me what you think about what I've said.

Your mom and I have always tried to teach you what we believe is God's truth about sex. When a man and a woman grow to love each other and choose to get married, their bodies are one part of the wonderful way God made them able to join as husband and wife. A husband and wife are sharing their bodies completely when their bodies are fitted together by the man's penis being in the woman's vagina in sexual intercourse. Sharing their bodies should draw them closer to each other and help build their love. Your mom and I are strongly connected to each other, and part of that is because we have sexual intercourse with each other.

God thinks sexual intercourse is so special that he wants us to keep it only for marriage. He wants us to be filled with love for each other, and only for each other. God wants marriage to last as long as you live. It doesn't always work out that way. Lots of people are divorced. But God wants a man and woman to have a beautiful life together for as long as they live.

Some people break God's law by having sex before they get married. They have sex with people they are not married to. Other people break God's law even when they are married by having sex with someone other than their husband or wife. This makes God very sad. Sex is so special in God's eyes that he wants us to keep it only for the person we are married to.

SAM: *But what does this have to do with movies?*

DAD: I'm taking a while to get there, aren't I? Okay. Movies and TV programs that show people jumping into bed with each other while wearing little or no clothes, as well as advertisements in magazines and on billboards that show women or men with hardly any clothes on or no clothes on at all, are trying to teach you something about sex.

SAM: *Teach me about sex? What do you mean? Movies are fun; it's not school!*

DAD: Yes and no. Suppose there is a movie that has lots of good chase scenes and car wrecks and so forth, but it also shows a man and a woman meeting for the first time, sort of liking each other even though they don't really know each other, and then they immediately start having sex. The people who made the movie make the two people look really beautiful, and filmmakers play just the right music and show just the right things to make it seem very exciting.

And then after the people have sex (though they are really just actors), it shows them feeling happy about what they did, and there are no problems whatsoever from what they chose to do. Now, what do you think something like that would teach a young person like you who is watching that movie?

SAM: *Well, I guess it would teach me that what those two people did was okay. Maybe that it's something exciting to do?*

DAD: I think you are exactly right. When we watch a movie or a TV program, we sometimes forget that it's a made-up story. What we watch can really influence us. If it's a fantasy movie where we are seeing nothing but weird creatures from space, we are probably not very affected by it. But almost every movie and television program today shows the same thing: people having sex when they've barely met. It's always exciting and perfect and rarely has any negative consequences.

After watching these things over and over, we might really begin to believe that sex between people who have just met is wonderful;

that it is a good way to say "I like you" or "I love you"; that sex is always exciting; that people never get hurt by having sex, or get a disease, or get pregnant. We know this is a lie. Yet, if we watch such things all the time, we may find it harder to believe the truth.

SAM: *But I think I could handle it!*

DAD: Let me ask you a question: What would happen if you tried to lift weights that are too heavy for you?

SAM: *I guess I might think I could do it, but I could hurt myself trying. What does that have to do with movies?*

DAD: Think of it this way. You are sort of like an athlete who is facing the biggest contest of your life just a few years from now. I am your coach who is trying to help you build up your strength and endurance for that big contest. I would be a very poor coach if I let you take on too much at this point in your training.

If you try to lift weights that are too heavy for you, you can really hurt yourself, maybe even permanently. Maybe you will be able to handle those heavy weights later, but only if you work with lighter weights now. I want you to be ready for the big contest that is going to happen when you are a young adult. To give you the best chance to be ready for that big contest, I am trying to protect you now from anything that would make you less strong later. What do you think about that?

SOME QUESTIONS TO DISCUSS

1. What are some ways in which the programs and movies we watch and the things we read can change how we think about sex, God, family, and other things?

2. How are people hurt by looking at "dirty" pictures?

CHAPTER 9

Danger Ahead!

MOM: Sam, your dad told me about your wonderful conversation about why we don't let you see R-rated movies or watch anything that has a lot of nudity or sex in it. Now we want to talk to the two of you together about a very serious topic, pornography. Have you heard of that?

AMY: *I don't think so.*

SAM: *Sort of. I've heard guys whispering about seeing things on the Internet that were amazing and showed a lot of sex.*

DAD: Yes, that's the kind of thing we're talking about. We call it "pornography" because long ago in Greece, the word *porneia* or *porno* meant sexual filth or dirt, and *graphia* or *graphy* meant writing or pictures. So pornography means dirty pictures or stories. Pornography today is extremely dangerous. We want to warn you not to get involved with it and not to even let yourself see any of it at all.

SAM: *Is it that bad? One of the kids at school said he had seen videos like that on his dad's computer. He said that kids could look at it when they come over to his house. I didn't see it, but the kid that went over there said it was fantastic.*

DAD: Well, I'm glad you didn't do it! Let's think through the reasons why. First, do you remember discussing how movies that show people naked and stuff like that actually teach things about sex and even encourage actions that go against God's laws? Well, pornography does that, too, but it is much worse than that.

SAM: *Worse how?*

MOM: Well, first, the movies and TV shows mostly show people who at least know and care for each other having sex before they should. Pornography often shows things that are much worse, such as men treating women in awful ways. Instead of treating women with respect, as people made in the image of God, they treat women like things that can be used for their own pleasure. They show men making the women do things that no healthy woman really wants to do—things that God did not mean for the beautiful gift of a woman's body to be used for. Often, they show women pretending that they want the man to do these things to her.

AMY: *What kinds of things?!*

MOM: Some of the videos show men raping women and the women pretending that they like it. You know what rape is, right?

It's when a man forces a woman to have sex through violence or drugs or in any other way that's against her will. They show many other things as well, but you'll have to be older before we talk about them.

AMY: *But why would a woman pretend to like that?*

DAD: That's a very good question, Amy. Some of the women think so little of themselves or have had so much trouble in their lives that they believe that is the only way they can make money. Others twist things around in their minds until they convince themselves that they actually enjoy what is being done to them.

But many of the videos are done by women who are basically slaves. I'm very sad to say there are people in this world so evil that they will entrap runaways or even kidnap young women and literally force them to do these things. Men can get these images in their heads and expect their wives to behave like the actors, which is an insult to their wives.

Can you understand how different this is from what God meant sex to be? God means sex to be a beautiful thing that bonds a husband and wife together. The husband and wife voluntarily give their whole lives to each other. They have taken the time to get to know each other and love each other. Such people get married because they believe this is what God wants for them, that the marriage is God's gift to them. Nothing could be further from what pornographic videos show.

MOM: By watching such movies, boys and girls can begin believing that it's okay to treat a woman like an object or thing. Some of the women who act in those videos have basically let themselves be used as things for money. Others are pressured or forced against their will to do such things.

I think it is also true that boys who look at such pictures or videos all the time can begin thinking that there is only one way for a woman to be beautiful, and that is to have exactly the kind of body that is shown in the pictures or videos. Boys can begin believing that women should show off their bodies in those ways. I think this is ugly and destructive. And when that is what boys believe, girls can come to believe it too.

AMY: *They do?*

MOM: Yes. Amy, think about the way so many women dress who are on magazine covers that we see the grocery store. They are dressing—or undressing, really—to look sexy for everybody, to look like they're saying, "I'm beautiful and I'm ready to have sex with you" to all the men that see the picture.

Women are not things; we are not objects to be used. We are people made in God's image. We deserve to be treated as people. Many people who aren't Christians agree that pornography and some commercials on TV or ads in magazines create a lot of trouble for women. They lead men to look at women just for their bodies rather than as real people to love and respect.

DAD: And that brings me to another reason to stay away from pornography. Kids, you remember how we talked about staying away from drugs because they can be addictive? We now know that pornography can be addictive in a similar way.

AMY: *I know that drugs are bad, but I'm not sure what addictive means.*

DAD: God made our brains to feel and enjoy pleasure, including from sex. God meant this as a gift so that we could enjoy the good things he gives in the way he intended. Food and wine are other examples. Some people abuse God's gifts. Addiction is when one of God's gifts is misused so that it becomes hard to stop misusing it, which causes your life to get worse and worse and actually changes your body and brain to where you are almost a slave to what you are addicted to.

MOM: This is especially important for young people like you. From about the age of ten or eleven through the early twenties, your brains are especially quick at adapting to things like this. On the good side, this makes you great learners. On the downside, it makes you vulnerable to learning twisted, wrong, evil lessons that could haunt you for the rest your lives.

Boys and men who get involved in pornography find their brain changing to where they want more and more pornography. They slowly become less and less satisfied with other parts of their lives; things that used to be fun like playing games or getting to know a woman they like no longer make them happy. And while this happens, they become more isolated and lonely, do worse in school, have more trouble with their friendships, get depressed, and have all kinds of problems.

DAD: It makes your mom and me sad to have to talk to about this at all. It is because of the dangers of pornography that we are so careful about the time you spend on the computer, cell phone, and so forth. We're trying to protect you.

And speaking of protection, you both have to be especially careful of how you use a cell phone or tablet device. People who push pornography are often trying to get you to click on a link or download something onto the cell phone. Also, one type of pornography, sadly, happens when teenagers or even children foolishly choose to send naked or nearly naked pictures of themselves; this is called sexting. It is against the law and it's also a form of pornography.

SAM: *That all sounds terrible.*

MOM: We have talked about how pornography presents a distorted view of women, making them seem like things to be used rather than people to be respected. Pornography is often made with women forced against their will to do the things that are filmed. Pornography presents unhealthy, twisted, and evil sexual acts as exciting and pleasurable, and pornography can quickly become an addiction that is hard to stop and can ruin your lives for months or years.

Let me say two additional things. First, boys who watch pornography can begin to believe that this is how their future wives should act. As future husbands, they may pressure or even bully their wives into doing things that are not really loving or giving. Second, people who act in and make the pornography are violating God's laws of modesty and of keeping sex within marriage. So if you use pornography, you're supporting people doing things that make God very sad. He gets angry, too, because God hates when his good gifts are misused.

We pray you will grow strong in believing the right way about sex—God's way. Staying away from pornography is important!

SOME QUESTIONS TO DISCUSS

1. What is pornography? What is sexting?
2. What are the best ways for you to stay safe from pornography?
3. Why would God disapprove of the use of pornography?
4. How could the use of pornography affect your future marriage?

CHAPTER 10

What Does God Think about Gay People?

AMY: *Dad, what do people mean when they call someone "gay"? A boy at school said that his uncle is gay. Some of the kids giggled about it.*

DAD: Okay; I'll do my best to explain, and you can ask any questions you want.

Some men and women are homosexual. *Gay* is a word that some people use to describe a man who is homosexual. A woman who is a homosexual is called a lesbian. Some people use the word *gay* to describe both men and women who are homosexual.

Now let me tell you what the word *homosexual* means. I hope you can see how your mom and I love each other; we express that love physically by kissing and holding each other because we feel strong feelings of love for each other. God gave us the gift of sex to share together as the very closest we can get to each other physically. God made us so that it is natural to want to hug, kiss, and even have sex with the person you are attracted to. Most people are only attracted to and fall in love with people of the opposite sex—men with women and women with men. It is common today to call this being heterosexual. "Hetero" means other or different, so combined with "sexual," it means the person feels sexual feeling for the other sex.

But just because it is natural for most people doesn't mean that it always happens that way. "Homo" means same or alike. Homosexuals are people who find that they are attracted to or even fall in love with and want to kiss, hold, and have sex with people of the same sex. For example, a gay man is a man who desires sex with other men, but not with women. A lesbian is a woman who desires sex with other women, but not with a man. For them, that's what feels normal.

MOM: Some other people describe themselves as bisexual, which means they are attracted to both men and women. Sometimes when people talk about folks who are "gay," they mean everyone who's not heterosexual.

AMY: *But wait a minute! You told me that having sex meant that a man's penis goes into a woman's vagina. How can a man have sex with another man when neither of them has a vagina? And how can a woman have sex with another woman when neither of them has a penis?*

DAD: That is a great question, but I can't give you a complete answer because it is too complicated for you at your age. The basic answer is that they cannot have sexual intercourse the way a husband and wife do, and so they find other ways to stimulate each other's genitals so that they feel good. And some of them say that this is just as good as sexual intercourse for them.

AMY: *But is it bad to be gay? I have heard people in our church talk about gay people as if that is really bad. Are they right?*

DAD: Well, that depends on what you mean by really bad. Your mom and I believe that the Bible teaches that all of us have bad in us. Romans 3:23 says that "all have sinned and fall short of the glory of God." Everyone has sinned. That means you and I are just as much of a sinner as any gay or lesbian person, and that is a really bad thing.

When we say that someone is a bad person, we often mean that the person does bad things all the time, or even that the person enjoys being really evil and never misses an opportunity to do something that is wrong. But most gay or lesbian people are not this way any more than most husbands or wives are this way. Many homosexual people are kind, hardworking, truthful, or show other good ways of behaving. And all homosexual people were made in God's image and deserve to be treated with dignity.

It is still true, though, that God does not want men to have sex with men, or women with women. The Bible doesn't talk a lot about people acting like homosexuals. But in those few places where it does, the Bible describes it as something that God does not want people to do. For example, Leviticus 18:22 says, "You shall not lie with a male as with a woman; it is an abomination." Clearly, this is something God does not want us to do.

And 1 Corinthians 6:9-10 says, "Do you not know that the unrighteous will not inherit the kingdom of God? Do not be deceived: neither the sexually immoral, nor idolaters, nor adulterers, nor men who practice homosexuality, nor thieves, nor the greedy, nor drunkards, nor revilers, nor swindlers will inherit the kingdom of God."

SAM: *So gay people can't go to heaven?*

DAD: No, that is not what it means. As I understand it, this means that we show who we love by what we do. Some people continue to break God's rules by doing things God says not to do. Those people are showing in their actions that they don't really love God or accept Jesus as their Lord and Savior. That is why your mom and I think that it is a bad choice for people to have sex outside of a marriage between a man and a woman.

The Bible teaches that God meant for us to fall in love with, marry, and have sex with a person different from us—a woman with a man and a man with a woman. That way, we can have children. That way, we can show the world in our marriages what God's love is like. If we don't get married, for whatever the reason, God wants us to not have sex but to remain a virgin, a person who has never had sex. A single person living a life devoted to God is a model of God's love and faithfulness for the world in the same way.

AMY: *But why is anyone homosexual?*

DAD: That may be the hardest question of all. Maybe you are really asking two questions: Why do people feel that way? And why do people act that way?

Why do people feel that way? It seems like most homosexual people don't just choose to feel that way. Many say they grew up with those feelings. No one knows for sure why some people feel this way when they are adults. A lot of people today say that science has proven that homosexuals are born that way, but actually, the best scientists say we really don't know.

AMY: *What if I ever feel that way?*

DAD: I think the most important thing is for you not to worry about feeling that way. It is sad so many kids worry needlessly about whether they will become homosexual. Not very many people are homosexual; most scientists who study this issue today say that only about 3 to 4 percent of people—only three or four people out of every one hundred—are homosexual.

When you go through puberty and are a young man or a young woman, you will have lots of feelings that are hard to explain and that you are not very comfortable with. Lots of people have feelings that seem like homosexual feelings when they are teenagers, but they grow up to feel the normal feelings for a husband or wife. The teen years are full of strong feelings that don't last.

One specific example might be a girl who has a friend that she really likes and who is really quite beautiful. They might be together at a party or a sports event or a youth group meeting, and when something exciting happens, they spontaneously hug each other. With all the talk about sexuality today, the girl might confuse the affection and joy of friendship and the pleasure of hugging a person you really care about with homosexual feelings. There are a lot of labels that are applied today to feelings that are just part of the spectrum of normal feelings kids have in puberty.

I think you can expect and not worry about any troubling feelings you might have in your teenage years, but I would ask you to come talk with me about anything that worries you. It can help just to talk about it. Most of us go through a rocky period when we're young. It feels like our bodies and our emotions don't make sense, but we must go through it so that we can grow into the adult God wants us to be.

AMY: *What if someone feels like a homosexual? Does that mean they have to have sex with another homosexual?*

DAD: There are Christian men and women who feel those feelings and choose to obey God by not having sex at all. This is the way God wants all people who are not married to behave, and many Christian men and women now and throughout history have lived beautiful lives like this. And there are some people who have such feelings or even lived as a homosexual for a while, and then God healed them so that they could have a normal marriage.

But there are many homosexuals who act as homosexuals, who "live the gay lifestyle." God does not want this, but they do it anyway. Some do it because they do not believe in God or his rules, and they think that if sex is only for pleasure, they can have sex with anyone they want. Some believe in God and in Jesus but believe that the Bible is wrong in what it teaches about how they should act, or they claim it doesn't really teach that this is wrong. Some do it because they need someone to love, and the only person or people they can find to love are other homosexuals. Some do it because their lives are very empty and sex is the only joy or reason they can find to live.

SAM: *But if it's wrong, why can gay people get married?*

MOM: Sam, for many years most of the people in our country were Christians, and so they assumed that marriage was only for one man and one woman. They made laws on that assumption. With fewer Christians, more and more people began believing that sex was for anyone who wanted to do it and that there is no reason for the government to stop people from getting married, even if they're the same sex. So the Supreme Court said that gay and lesbian people can get married too. But we believe the Bible teaches that only one man and one woman can get and be married.

You and I need to remember that God loves homosexual people. Jesus died for them just as he died for you and me. We do not agree with what they are doing; God says it is wrong to live as a homosexual. But they should be treated like all other people, with great love and great respect.

SOME QUESTIONS TO DISCUSS

1. What is a homosexual?
2. What does the Bible say about two men or two women having sex together?
3. Does God's disapproval of gay sex mean that gay, lesbian, and other people are awful, mean, or completely evil people?
4. How would God have you behave toward such people?

CHAPTER 11

What Is Sexual Abuse?

DAD: Kids, I want to talk to you about what adults call "sexual abuse." Have you ever heard that term?

SAM: *I think so, Dad, but I'm not sure what it means.*

DAD: Well, it seems to be in the news a lot these days. Do you remember when we had the TV news on last night while we were putting dinner on the table? The reporter talked about a coach who had sexually abused some children. I thought it would be good for us to talk about the subject.

AMY: *Yeah, what did that mean?*

DAD: We talked before about how God made our bodies and our sexuality for us to enjoy, but that God means for marriage to be the only place where we experience sexual intercourse and the full sharing of our bodies. This is why God set up his rule that two people should not have sex unless they are married. God hopes this rule will protect us against misusing the marvelous gift that he gave us by making our bodies. People break these rules in all sorts of ways and for all sorts of reasons.

MOM: One of the ways people break God's rules is through sexual abuse. The phrase *sexual abuse* refers to an adult or older kid, like a teenager, using a child's body for the adult's or older kid's sexual pleasure. And I want to be clear: The one breaking God's rules when this happens is not the younger child; it is the older person taking advantage of the younger child by abusing him or her.

AMY: *But Mom, what does that mean, to abuse someone?*

MOM: I hate even talking about it, because the very thought of it makes me upset, sad, and angry at the same time. But it is important to talk about, because I want to protect you and teach you to protect yourself.

Sexual abuse can happen to kids of all ages. It can happen to a baby or a child who is only two or three. It can happen to a sixteen- or seventeen-year-old girl or boy. Sexual abuse can happen when a grown-up or even an older child kisses or touches a younger child, like if an older kid forced you to kiss him, or an adult put his hand between your legs to touch your vagina, Amy, or your penis, Sam. Another type of sexual abuse can be when an adult or older child forces a child to touch the adult's genitals or other parts of his body in a sexual way. Or sexual abuse can be when a person shows his sexual organs—his private parts—to the child, or even if he shows the child pictures of naked people or some other type of pornography. And sometimes it can mean the adult actually having sexual intercourse with the child. That's called rape, which is any kind of sexual intercourse between an adult and a child, or when one adult forces another adult to have sex when she or he is not willing.

SAM: *That's gross!*

DAD: It's gross and it is evil, Sam. We don't want to frighten you by telling you this. We want to tell you so you can protect yourself and we can protect you better. The people who commit acts of sexual abuse are almost always men. Most of the time, girls are the ones who are abused, but sexual abuse is also directed at boys sometimes. That's why we wanted to talk to both of you.

SAM: *But why would someone do that?*

DAD: People do what we call sexual abuse for a lot of different reasons. People who hate God and want to do what is bad instead of good will sometimes look at God's rules and then try to do the worst possible things they can to break those rules. So it is possible that some people who engage in sexual abuse do so because of evil in their hearts.

Some people do it because of horrible things that happened to them when they were growing up. Maybe they were sexually abused themselves. These sorts of things can really twist people's hearts and minds so that it feels more natural to them to be sexually interested in a child than in an adult. Other people might be so lonely or depressed or confused that they sexually abuse a child as a way to forget their unhappiness. There are probably other reasons as well.

AMY: *But what are you supposed to do about it? How do you keep it from happening?*

DAD: I'm really glad you asked that question, because that is exactly what I was going to talk about next. I want you to understand that not everything that is unpleasant is sexual abuse. Remember years ago when you were little and you came in crying because the little boy up the street pulled his underwear down and wiggled his rear end at you? That was rude, but it wasn't really sexual abuse. And you remember how at the last family reunion your great Aunt Liddy, bless her soul, grabbed your little sister and smothered her with kisses even though she was fighting to get away? Well, that wasn't sexual abuse either.

SAM: *Then how can you tell what is sexual abuse?*

MOM: There are four important things that we would like you to remember.

First, remember that it is an absolute rule that no one has the right to see or touch the private parts of your body—the genital area for boys and the breasts and the genital area for girls—except a doctor who is examining you and your parents under certain circumstances, like if you are hurt or something. If anyone tries to make you do either of those things—to see and touch you or to have you see and touch that person—you should immediately try to get out of the situation and tell us right away so that we can help you decide what to do. It is our job as parents to protect you.

The second rule is that you should trust your feelings about what you like and feel comfortable with and what you don't like and don't feel comfortable with. For instance, suppose one of your friends had a real "kissy" family, and after a while, someone in that family gave you a kiss. A little kiss itself is not sexual abuse, but if that kiss isn't comfortable for you, and if we talk about it and we're not comfortable about it either, then it is like sexual abuse if that person keeps doing it after we ask him or her to stop.

Third, do not get into sexual conversations, whether with strangers or with older kids or adults, other than us. Older people sometimes hunt for younger kids on the Internet through e-mail, social media, or forums. They might even pretend to be other kids! And sometimes adults will do the same thing in person or by phone. They start the conversation on other things and then patiently but steadily try to get you talking about your body, or what teenagers are doing sexually, and so forth. They manipulate kids into talking about sex to feel cool. Sometimes it is just talk, but some try to get kids to meet them so they can abuse them. You can stay safe by never letting such conversations happen and by always telling us if this happens.

The fourth thing is that you should not keep secrets from us about these kinds of things, not ever. If anything ever happens that makes you feel uncomfortable, you should tell us right away. We are here to protect you, but we can only protect you if we know what is going on.

Can you remember these four rules?

SAM: *Uh . . . never keep secrets, and don't talk about sex with strangers or other adults, and . . .*

AMY: *And keep our private areas private and trust our feelings that if something doesn't feel right, then it isn't!*

MOM: You guys are an awesome team! Now, it is very important for you to know that you can protect yourself against sexual abuse. The best thing is to be very strong and confident that you know what is right and wrong. Also, you must know that you will get our help in dealing with anything bad that happens to you. If anyone ever tries to kiss you or touch you or get you to do something that you are not completely sure is right, you should speak very strongly and say, "I am not going to do that, and I am going to talk to my mother and father about this." If anyone ever begs you not to tell us or even threatens you, don't believe what they say; they are lying. Sometimes sexual abusers make up stories about how they work for the police and that if a child tells his or her mom and dad, the police will get the mother and father in trouble. The person may even threaten to hurt the mother and father. Don't believe it. They are only lying to scare you and get what they want. We can protect ourselves, and we can protect you. So, no secrets like that—ever!

AMY: *But how do kids feel if something like that has happened to them? What happens to children who get sexually abused?*

MOM: Sexual abuse can make the child very sad and very upset for a long time. The most important thing is for the child to talk with his or her mother and father about it so that they can help decide what is best to do. Sometimes it helps a child to talk to a doctor or counselor about what happened. It may be very important for the people who did the sexual abuse to get arrested and go to jail as a way of punishing them and stopping them from hurting anybody else.

Another important thing is for a child to realize that it was not her or his fault. People who do such abuse try to make the child feel like it was the child's fault. This is never true! It is never a child's fault when something like this happens.

DAD: Some older children commit sexual abuse because they themselves have been sexually abused. We know one family where the son was sexually abused when he was four. He was sexually abused by a seven-year-old neighbor. The seven-year-old had been shown very dirty, evil movies by an adult and had probably done some of the things that were shown in those movies with the adult. So this seven-year-old boy had terribly wrong ideas about sex and what he should do with his body. Then he carried out those ideas with the four-year-old. That seven-year-old boy needed help, and the grown-up who got him into that kind of behavior needed to be punished by sending him to jail.

We really want you two to be able to protect yourselves against sexual abuse, and we want you to be able to come to us for protection. If you can remember anything like this ever happening to you, we want to talk with you about it, because it was not your fault and it is not something that needs to be a secret. Often, things that we keep secret have a terrible effect on us. But when we talk about them, God can help us heal from what happened.

MOM: We've talked a lot about bad things that can happen. But remember that our sexuality is a wonderful and beautiful gift from God. Sexual abuse is an evil way that people use a wonderful gift to do wrong. My hope is that you can be protected from this because we have talked openly about it, and I certainly want to work hard to protect you. I want to help protect you so that you can go on to have a life where you honor God by the way that you handle being a man or a woman.

SOME QUESTIONS TO DISCUSS

1. What is sexual abuse?
2. Should you ever keep a secret about someone trying to touch you or abuse you?

CHAPTER 12

God's Response to Wrong

SAM: *Mom, what does God think about all the people who break his rules? Does God get really mad at them? Does he hate them?*

MOM: That is such a good question. It shows how much you're thinking about the things we're trying to teach you.

You know how when you do something bad, I sometimes get angry at you? Like when I've told you several times not to horse around at the table but you do it again and spill your drink all over the table? I get furious. But even when I'm angry, do you think I stop loving you?

SAM: *Well, no, but when you're angry, I don't feel so loved.*

MOM: That's a good, honest answer. It may not show so much then, but even when I'm angry, I never stop loving you. God's love is much greater than ours, and he never stops loving us. The Bible says, "For God so loved the world, that he gave his only Son, that whoever believes in him should not perish but have eternal life" (John 3:16).

But it is still true that God gets angry when we sin. The Bible is full of verses that show us how angry God gets when we disobey him. No matter how angry God gets with us, God is always ready to forgive us for our sins. That's why Jesus died on the cross for us. Because God is perfectly fair, he requires that evil deeds be punished. But because he loves us so much, he gave his own Son, Jesus, to the world. Jesus let himself be punished for all our sins so that we wouldn't have to be punished by God. Jesus was punished for us!

So God is always ready to forgive anyone who comes to him and sincerely asks to be forgiven. God is always ready to forgive people who misuse his gift of sexuality.

AMY: *If God will forgive us, does it really matter if we break his rules?*

DAD: Just because God will forgive us doesn't mean that we are free to break his rules. We all need to decide who we really love, who we are really serving. Jesus said, "If you love me, you will keep my commandments" (John 14:15). People who disobey Jesus' commands and break God's rules over and over again are showing in their actions that they don't really love God. This is why the decisions we make are so important, because they show what is really in our hearts.

When people do something that God hates, God is always willing to forgive them for what they have done. But forgiveness doesn't magically correct whatever has gone wrong because of our wrong choices. When you knock over your drink at dinner and I forgive you, the juice doesn't magically jump back off the table and chairs and go back into your glass. The same thing is true about sex.

Many bad things can happen because people have sex with each other. Sex outside of marriage is wrong because God tells us not to do it, and we ought to obey him. Sex outside of marriage is wrong because God made sex as a gift to bond a husband and wife together for life, and it is wrong to use that gift in any other way. But having sex outside of marriage is also wrong because of the terribly bad things that can happen as a result. And God's forgiveness does not make these bad things disappear.

AMY: *Like the girl getting pregnant when she isn't married? That happened to a girl in our church, didn't it?*

MOM: Right! Yes, any woman who has sex, married or not, can get pregnant. Let's think about pregnancy for a girl. If a fifteen-year-old girl has sex, she is taking a chance on getting pregnant. She may feel bad about having sex and may pray to God for forgiveness. I believe God will forgive her if she sincerely asks for that forgiveness, but she still may be pregnant. If she is pregnant, a doctor or counselor might suggest she think about getting an abortion. Hundreds of thousands of teenage girls get abortions each year. A doctor kills the tiny baby inside her because the girl has decided that a pregnancy and having a baby is not a good thing for her right then. So the first decision she might have to face is whether to get an abortion.

Your father and I believe this is wrong. A woman who has an abortion doesn't have to go through the pregnancy, but she has to live for the rest of her life with the knowledge of what she did to her own son or daughter that she was carrying inside her.

SAM: *But if she doesn't have an abortion, she has a baby, right? That would be hard.*

DAD: Yes, it's hard. If she decides not to have an abortion, she will have the baby after nine months. She may choose to give the baby for adoption to another loving family who can't have a baby of their own. This is a wonderful gift to them, but it is very hard to give up a baby the young mother has carried for nine months.

She may choose to keep the baby. Think of what this involves. She may have to drop out of school. She will have to go through watching her body change, grow larger, and give birth to a child, probably without a husband around to help. She will find it very difficult to go back to school after having a baby, because babies demand so much care and attention. She will desperately need money to take care of herself but will have a hard time getting a job because of the care that the baby needs and because she doesn't have a good education. She will need to care for that child for longer than she has been alive herself, for the next eighteen years. She will not fit in with her old friends anymore because they don't have children and can hardly understand why she can't do the things that she used to do.

SAM: *What about the baby's father?*

MOM: Good question. Neither the boy nor the girl usually intends for her to get pregnant, but there is always a chance of that happening. If he gets her pregnant, then he may have to participate in the decision of whether to have an abortion. What if he doesn't believe in abortion, but she gets one anyway? If she chooses not to have an abortion, he has to go through the whole decision about whether the two of them should marry or not. Marriages that start off because of a girl's pregnancy in the teenage years often are not very good marriages. Whether he marries her or not, he ought to help support the child that is born because of his having sex with the mother, because he is the father. This can result in a young man dropping out of high school and changing his life forever as well, even if he never marries the mother.

AMY: *That sounds awful!*

MOM: It is terribly hard on both the young mother and father.

DAD: And pregnancy is not the only difficult thing that can happen when people have sex outside of God's rules. People who have sex outside of marriage can also catch what are called sexually transmitted infections, abbreviated STIs. Some of these infections or diseases are fatal if untreated, and others have terrible consequences, such as leaving a woman unable to have children or strongly increasing the woman's chances of having cancer. Some of these diseases can be treated and cured. Others can never be cured; the best doctors can do is to help people live longer with fewer problems.

Kids, people who follow God's rules don't have to worry about these things. If we don't give our bodies to another person before we get married and have sex only with our spouse, and our spouse does the same, we have very little to be worried about.

SAM: *I saw a poster at the high school last month that said something about how these diseases could be prevented by using something called a condom. Is that true? What's a condom?*

MOM: Well, a condom looks a little bit like a balloon, though it is made of something different and tougher than a balloon is. The condom slips over a man's penis before he has sex so that his semen and the skin of his penis cannot touch the other person's body. This helps protect both of the people who are having sex from catching a sexual infection from each other because the skin of their genitals touch less and the man's semen is less likely to go in the woman's body. Using a condom also helps keep a woman from getting pregnant when she has sex, because the sperm in the man's semen doesn't get into her vagina and uterus. That is, it doesn't if the condom has been used correctly and doesn't break.

AMY: *It can break?*

DAD: Many people think that if they have sex wearing a condom, they are having "safe sex." And they think that as long as sex is safe, it is okay. They are wrong on both points. First, even if sex is safe, it's still wrong if the two people are not married. Even if no one gets pregnant or gets a disease from having sex, it's still wrong because it isn't what God wants and it isn't what God made sex for.

Second, sex is never completely "safe." People who use condoms do not get pregnant as much as people who don't, and people who use condoms do not get sexual diseases as much as people who don't. But they still get pregnant sometimes and they still get diseases sometimes because people don't use condoms correctly or the condoms break. So sex is never completely safe.

I think God must be really sad when he thinks about people catching diseases and ruining their future. God made sex to be a wonderful gift between a wife and her husband. People have so messed up this gift that sex now becomes the way that people infect each other with a disease that can kill them.

MOM: Well, we've talked about a lot of hard stuff, but you originally asked me if God hates the people who break his rules. The answer to that question is no. God never stops loving his children, even though their disobedience makes him very angry. But God does hate the bad things we do. We can be forgiven for the bad things we do, but our lives may be changed forever by the consequences of what we do. Even then, God can bring good out of the worst consequences, like when a person with an STI becomes a Christian and spends the rest of his or her life loving and serving God.

I pray that you will make choices that give God joy. You are in the process of becoming an adult. That means that more and more of your choices will be really big ones that can change your life forever. Of course, your choices matter now. If you spend all of fourth grade goofing off, you will have a harder time in fifth grade, and then you may not do as well in middle school. But in the years ahead, you will make decisions about things that could change your life for much longer than a year or two. For example, if you drink alcohol and drive when you are sixteen, you could get in an accident and be paralyzed for the rest of your life. Or if you decide to have sex before you are married, you could really hurt yourself and others. Part of growing up is realizing just how big many of the decisions you make really are. You are already making choices that will influence the rest of your life, and you have to choose whether to make choices that please God or ones that disappoint him.

SOME QUESTIONS TO DISCUSS

1. How can we know that God never stops loving us?
2. How can we express our love for God?
3. Is there such a thing as "safe sex"?
4. Does God's forgiveness take away the bad things that can happen when we make wrong, sinful choices?

CHAPTER 13

Growing Up

AMY: *Mom and Dad, I've been thinking about some of the stuff we've been talking with you guys about. About sex and stuff. I don't know if I can say it right, but I guess I'm not sure I want to grow up. I mean, you say sex is a wonderful gift and all that, but it seems like there are some things to be scared about when you're a grown-up. I'm not sure I'm ready for that.*

SAM: *I feel that way too! I'd like to be married someday, I think, but it doesn't sound as easy or as fun as I thought it would be.*

MOM: I think I understand just what you mean. You aren't ready to handle some of these things yet, and that makes them sound really scary. The reason we are talking about them with you now is to help you be ready when it is time for you to make decisions, like if another kid asks you to watch pornography on the Internet, or when there's a boy or girl you really like when you are a teenager. Everyone is a bit scared of handling situations and making decisions that he or she has never faced before, even grown-ups. By talking about it ahead of time, we help get ready to make those decisions. Did you know your dad and I were excited but scared about having kids? Talking about what it would be like to have kids and how we might handle some tough situations really helped us get ready to be parents.

DAD: I agree. Also, as we live in our family and have our nice friends and go to church, it can seem like everything happens so easily and naturally. But the world is a scary place, even for us adults. Everyone has to face problems. Some problems, like sexually transmitted diseases and unwanted pregnancies, are caused by making bad choices that break God's rules for our lives. But even faithful Christians face problems, like a wife whose husband has an affair with another woman, or when others say Christians are stupid or outdated to think God doesn't want us to have sex before we are married.

That's why we must have courage. Courage is when we have the strength to do what is right even when we're nervous or scared. God can give us that courage. If we trust God, believe that he tells us the truth in the Bible, and ask him to forgive us and help us do what is right, we believe God will answer that prayer. He will give us the courage and the strength to do what is right. I wish being a Christian was easy, but it never has been easy. And many Christians have had to face a much more difficult world than we do!

AMY: *But is it worth it to grow up? With all the problems in the world?*

DAD: Yes it is, Amy. I had a wonderful childhood, filled with a lot of joy. I hope your childhood is even better. Some people aren't as fortunate and look back on many difficult times in childhood. But even so, the joys of being an adult are special. The hard parts about being an adult make the good things that much more wonderful.

And sexuality is part of that. My love for Christ is the most important thing in my life. But next to God, I love your mother and you kids the most. You guys make my life full of joy! And without sexuality, there would be no marriage, no children, no families. I'm glad you love being a child, but in a few more years, you will feel ready to move on to becoming an adult; you'll be ready to trade in the joys of childhood for the deeper and more complicated joys of adulthood.

MOM: And when you are ready, I hope that having talked about sex in our family will help you make the right decisions. One of the wonderful things about the Christian faith is that we can trust that God helps us with the toughest decisions of our lives by showing us the right way in the Bible, the way he wants us to live.

But another wonderful thing about the Christian faith is that our God never stops loving us, even when we make wrong decisions. He can forgive us for what we did wrong and help us rebuild our lives. It's better to make the right decision in the first place, because then we don't have as much painful rebuilding to do! But isn't it wonderful that our Lord is so full of forgiveness and truth?

SAM: *And I guess there's nothing we can do about it, anyway. We can't stay kids.*

MOM: That's right! So enjoy being kids! And talk with us about anything that you wonder about or that bothers you. It is a joy, a privilege, to talk with you guys about these things. We are always ready to talk and pray with you.

SOME QUESTIONS TO DISCUSS

1. How do you feel about growing up—excited, scared, confident, or what?

2. How does talking to your mom or dad about sex feel to you?

NOTES

1. Stanton L. Jones, "How to Teach Sex: Seven Realities That Christians in Every Congregation Need to Know," *Christianity Today* 55, no. 1 (January 2011): 34–39.
2. For images and a detailed summary of female biological processes, please go to http://www.christiansexed.com/bringing-the-biology-together/.
3. For images and a detailed summary of male biological processes, please go to http://www.christiansexed.com/bringing-the-biology-together/.

ABOUT THE AUTHORS

STAN (STANTON L.) JONES, PHD, is a clinical psychologist. He recently returned to serving as professor of psychology at Wheaton College after serving for twenty years as its provost (chief academic officer). Earlier, he led in establishing Wheaton's PsyD program in clinical psychology. He has been a visiting scholar at the University of Cambridge and has published many articles in journals such as *American Psychologist, General Psychologist, First Things*, and *Christianity Today*. Beyond the God's Design for Sex series, his books include *Psychology: A Student's Guide, Modern Psychotherapies: A Comprehensive Christian Appraisal* (2nd ed., with Richard E. Butman), *Ex-Gays?: A Longitudinal Study of Religiously Mediated Change in Sexual Orientation* (with Mark A. Yarhouse), and *Homosexuality: The Use of Scientific Research in the Church's Moral Debate* (with Mark A. Yarhouse).

BRENNA JONES serves in a professional ministry of discipleship and support as well as spiritual counsel and prayer for women. She served as a leader in a Bible-study ministry with women for a number of years. She has graduate training in biblical and theological studies.

BRENNA AND STAN wrote the original versions of their books on sex education while their three children were young; now they enjoy their three kids as adults, along with their kids' spouses and children.